W9-CPE-608

A CULTURAL HISTORY OF WOMEN IN AMERICA

THE GREAT DEPRESSION: THE JAZZ AGE, PROHIBITION, AND ECONOMIC DECLINE 1921–1937

JANE BINGHAM

CHELSEA HOUSE

An Infobase Learning Company

THE GREAT DEPRESSION: THE JAZZ AGE, PROHIBITION, AND ECONOMIC DECLINE 1921–1937

Copyright © 2011 Bailey Publishing Associates Ltd

Produced for Chelsea House by Bailey Publishing Associates Ltd, 11a Woodlands, Hove BN3 6TJ, England

Library of Congress Cataloging-in-Publication Data
Bingham, Jane.
  The Great Depression : the Jazz Age, Prohibition, and the Great Depression, 1921–1937 / Jane Bingham.
    p. cm. — (A cultural history of women in America)
  Includes index.
  ISBN 978-1-60413-933-4
  1. Women—United States—Social conditions—20th century. 2. Women—United States—History—20th century. 3. Depressions—1929—United States. 4. United States—Social conditions—1933–1945. 5. United States—History—1933–1945. I. Title.
  HQ1420.B49 2011
  973.91—dc22
                            2010044889

Chelsea House books are available at special discounts when purchased in bulk quantities for businesses, associations, institutions, or sales promotions. Please call our Special Sales Department in New York at (212) 967-8800 or (800) 322-8755.

You can find Chelsea House on the World Wide Web at: http://www.chelseahouse.com

Project management by Patience Coster
Text design by Jane Hawkins
Picture research by Shelley Noronha
Printed and bound in Malaysia
Bound book date: April 2011

10 9 8 7 6 5 4 3 2 1

This book is printed on acid-free paper.

All links and Web addresses were checked and verified to be correct at the time of publication. Because of the dynamic nature of the Web, some addresses and links may have changed since publication and may no longer be valid.

The publishers would like to thank the following for permission to reproduce their pictures:
The Art Archive: 5 (Culver Pictures), 16 (National Archives, Washington D.C.), 17 (National Archives, Washington D.C.), 18 (Willard Culver/NGS Image Collection), 26 (Willard Culver/NGS Image Collection); Corbis: 6 (Condé Nast Archive), 13, 20 (Bettmann), 23 (Bettmann), 25 (Minnesota Historical Society), 28 (Hulton-Deutsch Collection), 31 (Bettmann), 37 (Underwood & Underwood), 51 (Bettmann), 52, 53, 54, 56 (Bettmann), 58, 59 (Bettmann); Getty Images: 22, 44, 48, 50 (Time & Life Pictures); The Kobal Collection: 11; Rex Features: 7 (Everett Collection), 9 (Everett Collection), 21 (Everett Collection), 24 (Everett Collection), 30 (Everett Collection), 38 (GTV Archive), 40 (Everett Collection), 41 (Everett Collection), 43 (Everett Collection), 45 (ITV), 57 (Everett Collection); TopFoto: 8 (Roger-Viollet), 10 (Granger Collection), 12 (Granger Collection), 14, 15 (Granger Collection), 27 (Granger Collection), 29 (Granger Collection), 32 (Granger Collection), 33 (Granger Collection), 34, 35 (Ullstein Bild), 36, 39 (Granger Collection), 42 (ArenaPal), 46 (Granger Collection), 47 (Granger Collection), 49 (Granger Collection), 55 (Granger Collection); UNC Chapel-Hill-NC Collection: 19.

CONTENTS

Between the years 1921 and 1937, many American women experienced a dramatic turnaround in their way of life. In the early 1920s, some had well-paying jobs and enjoyed more freedom than women had ever known before. However, the good times came to an end in 1929 as banks and businesses began to fail. Over the next five years, there was a massive economic slump known as the Great Depression. Life became extremely hard for working women, wives, and mothers.

This book concentrates on key areas of women's lives, such as their role in the family and the workplace. It traces the growing role of women in politics after they gained the vote in 1920 and describes the part some women played in advancing learning and science, sports, and the arts.

The United States was a place of great social contrast in the 1920s and 1930s. This book surveys the lives of both rich and poor women. Chapter 7 looks at less privileged groups, such as African Americans, Native Americans and Hispanics, and shows how women celebrated their distinctive cultures in movements such as the Harlem Renaissance.

Right: In addition to being a pilot, Earhart wrote best-selling books about her flying experiences, designed a stylish range of clothes, and campaigned for votes for women.

TURNING POINT

SOLO FLIGHT

In 1932, at age thirty-four, Amelia Earhart became the first woman to fly an aircraft solo across the Atlantic. Her achievement proved that women could perform just as well as men and could achieve great things in exciting new areas of modern life. Earhart inspired a generation of young women to have the determination and courage to follow their dreams.

CHAPTER I

BOOM AND BUST

IN THE EARLY 1920S, THE UNITED STATES enjoyed a period of prosperity, but this was followed by the severe economic slump known as the Great Depression. By the late 1930s, however, life had begun to improve for many people. This was partly a result of the efforts of President Franklin Delano Roosevelt and his radical recovery program, known as the New Deal. In the wider world, some major social changes took place in the 1930s as communism and fascism emerged as significant political movements.

> ⤴ **TURNING POINT**

THE "TALKIES" ARRIVE

In 1927, the movie production company Warner Brothers released *The Jazz Singer*, which was shown in theaters around the United States. Although the movie was mostly silent, it was the first full-length feature film to include talking sequences. The launch of *The Jazz Singer* marked the end of the silent era and the start of movies with sound, nicknamed the "talkies."

Right: In the Roaring Twenties, some wealthy young women enjoyed a glamorous lifestyle, travelling in chauffeur-driven automobiles.

THE ROARING TWENTIES

The years between 1920 and 1929 are sometimes known as the "Roaring Twenties" or the "Jazz Age." During these exciting years, businesses boomed and art, music, theater, and film all blossomed. Jazz music was very popular, and movies became big business. Young women

were more independent than ever before and wore daring new fashions and makeup to emphasize their freedom. The rapid improvements in technology gave many people the chance to travel, and families began to own small automobiles.

PROHIBITION

During the 1920s, there was a nationwide attempt to overcome the many social problems caused by the excessive drinking of alcohol. Since the start of the 20th century, members of the temperance movement had campaigned to ban all alcohol, and in 1920, a national law was passed to prohibit the making or sale of intoxicating drink. The ban, which was known as Prohibition, proved extremely difficult to enforce. Alcohol was made and sold secretly, and illegal bars, known as speakeasies, sprang up in cities all over the United States. Prohibition was finally abandoned in 1933.

THE GREAT DEPRESSION

The Great Depression began in 1929 with a dramatic event called the Wall Street Crash. This led to the failure of banks and businesses all over the United States. Millions of people lost all their savings and their jobs, and thousands became homeless because they could not afford

Below: Crowds of investors gather outside banks on Wall Street, the commercial heart of New York City, on Black Tuesday.

TURNING POINT

THE WALL STREET CRASH

On October 29, 1929, the New York Stock Exchange on Wall Street announced that American share prices had dropped to almost zero. During the 1920s, many Americans had bought shares in businesses, hoping to make money by selling the shares at a higher price. However, in October 1929, share prices began to fall. People panicked and began selling their shares, which made prices drop even lower. On "Black Tuesday," the stock market collapsed. Many Americans realized they had lost all their savings, and businesses recognized they could no longer survive. This marked the start of the Great Depression, which quickly spread around the world.

Above: The extreme conditions of the Dust Bowl were partly caused by bad farming practices. For decades, farmers had plowed up the natural grasses that held the soil in place and kept moisture in the ground.

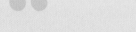

A CURTAIN OF BLACK

"On the fourteenth day of April of 1935
There struck the worst of dust storms
that ever filled the sky . . .
From Oklahoma City to the Arizona Line
Dakota and Nebraska to the lazy Rio
Grande
It fell across our city like a curtain of
black rolled down,
We thought it was our judgment, we
thought it was our doom . . . "

Lyrics from "The Great Dust Storm,"
by folk singer Woody Guthrie, 1940

to pay their rent. Some homeless families lived in shacks made of cardboard. Others took to the road in search of work.

THE DUST BOWL

Farmers were hit hard in the Great Depression as crop prices fell by more than half. To make matters worse, a series of severe droughts led to very poor harvests in the 1930s. In the Great Plains of central and western America, the soil turned to dust that was swept in choking black clouds for hundreds of miles. The problem affected Texas and Oklahoma and parts of New Mexico, Colorado, Minnesota, and Kansas, an area that became known as "the Dust Bowl." Millions of acres of farmland became useless, and hundreds of thousands of people were forced to leave their homes. Many of these families traveled west to California, where they struggled to find work.

THE NEW DEAL

The U.S. government took dramatic steps to help the country recover from the effects of the Great Depression and the Dust Bowl. This campaign of recovery was led by Franklin D. Roosevelt, who was elected president in 1932. Roosevelt introduced measures to support the poor, reform the banking system, and provide jobs. He also set up programs to encourage writers, musicians, and artists. Roosevelt's measures, which were known as the New Deal, helped to improve the fortunes of the United States. By the late 1930s, the nation was emerging from economic depression.

WORLD EVENTS

The period from 1921 to 1937 was a time of major social change in many parts of the world. In 1928, Joseph Stalin gained control of the communist Soviet Union and introduced a dictatorship, sending all his opponents to prison camps. In 1934, Chinese communist leader Mao Zedong led thousands of peasants on a 5,000-mile journey (known as the Long March) to escape Chinese nationalist forces. The Long March began Mao's rise to power, after which he would emerge as leader of the People's Republic of China.

While communist leaders controlled the Soviet Union and China, Adolf Hitler rose to power in Germany, becoming chancellor (head of the government) in 1933. Hitler's Nazi Party was made up of fascists who believed in total government control and claimed that the German race was superior to all others. They banned all political parties apart from their own and seized control of the media. Anyone who dared to disagree with the Nazis was instantly arrested, and Hitler launched a cruel campaign to persecute Jews, Gypsies and disabled people. By the late 1930s, Hitler was making plans to invade neighboring countries. Many people feared that war would be the only way to stop the spread of fascism.

WOMEN OF COURAGE AND CONVICTION

ELEANOR ROOSEVELT (1884–1962)

Eleanor Roosevelt was the first lady of the United States from 1933 to 1945. She supported the New Deal policies of her husband, Franklin D. Roosevelt, and was especially involved in rehousing projects and providing relief for the poor. Eleanor Roosevelt traveled across the United States giving speeches of support and organizing aid. She helped with campaigns for workers' rights and was especially active in the struggle of black women to gain full civil rights.

Below: Eleanor Roosevelt (right) with women and children in a soup kitchen during the Depression years. The slump saw many families relying on government aid for their survival.

CHAPTER 2

FAMILY LIFE AND SOCIAL ISSUES

DURING THE ROARING TWENTIES, MANY AMERICAN WOMEN experienced a rise in their standard of living, and some enjoyed an exciting new sense of freedom. In sharp contrast to this, life was extremely hard for women from poor families, who received almost no support from the government. With the start of the Great Depression in 1929, social problems became very severe, with millions of people unemployed and thousands homeless. Some determined female campaigners devoted themselves to improving the lives of the poor.

GAINING INDEPENDENCE

By the 1920s, most American girls received a basic high-school education, while women represented more than a third of all college students. These young women expected to use their education in some kind of job—at least until they married. At the same time, the rapid growth of businesses and cities in the 1920s provided new employment for female workers. Many young women worked in offices and stores, and some of them earned good wages, which they spent on clothes and entertainment.

FREEDOM AND FUN

Some single young women reveled in their freedom in the 1920s. They

Left: In the 1920s, the energetic dance known as the Charleston became popular across the United States.

CLARA BOW (1905–65)

Clara Bow grew up in poverty in Brooklyn, New York, and spent most of her childhood caring for her mentally ill mother. At the age of sixteen, she won a talent contest that launched her movie career. Between the years 1922 and 1933, Bow starred in fifty-eight films, but her greatest success was the movie *It*, in which she played a fun-loving shopgirl. Bow retired from the movies at age twenty-eight, and later suffered from many health problems. She is considered to be America's first sex symbol.

Left: With her daring haircut and "dangerous eyes," Clara Bow was the original "it girl."

wore short skirts, had their hair cut in a bob, and shocked the older generation by smoking cigarettes, drinking alcohol, and staying up late. These independent working women were sometimes nicknamed "flappers" and known as "it girls," after a movie called *It* starring Clara Bow as a young shopgirl, which was a massive hit in 1927. "It" referred to Bow's magnetic sex appeal, but the term came to be used for flappers in general. Along with their relaxed attitudes toward sexual relations, flappers enjoyed listening and dancing to jazz and learned new dances such as the Charleston. Some of the richer girls even drove their own automobiles.

MARRIAGE AND DIVORCE

By the start of the 20th century, attitudes to marriage were beginning to change. Girls were no longer expected to marry in their teens. Many chose to have a career before marriage, and some career women made a deliberate choice to stay single. Some high-profile women, such as journalist Dorothy Day, campaigned for a more relaxed attitude to relationships outside marriage. However, the majority of American women still held conventional ideas about marriage. Divorce became more common in the United States, but

TURNING POINT

THE ABDICATION OF EDWARD VIII

In 1936, British king Edward VIII announced he was abdicating (giving up his right to the throne) in order to marry an American divorcée named Wallis Simpson. Mrs Simpson had been married and divorced twice, and Edward recognized that British society could never accept her as his queen. In the United States, the majority of people believed that Edward was right to abdicate and that a divorced woman should not be allowed to hold such an important public position. The abdication showed that although divorce was becoming more common, it was still not generally accepted.

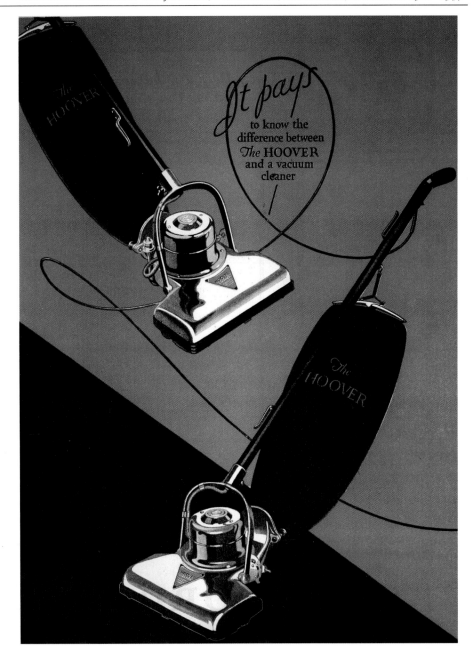

Left: The invention of the vacuum cleaner meant that women no longer had to clean floors on their hands and knees.

it was still very rare. Most people still considered divorce as a serious source of shame.

LIFE AT HOME

Only a small proportion of women could enjoy the "it girl" lifestyle. For most women in the 1920s and 1930s, life was based around the home. A woman's role was to be a supportive wife to her husband, to bring up the children, and to run the family home. This involved the time-consuming tasks of cooking, cleaning, and laundry. By the 1920s, the number of domestic servants had dropped dramatically, so most women had to do these tasks themselves.

A range of domestic appliances were marketed to help the housewife in her daily tasks. Washing machines, vacuum cleaners, and electric irons were all designed to make women's lives easier, but even with this new equipment, most housewives worked long, hard days to keep their houses clean and their families clothed and fed.

HELPING WORKING WOMEN

Some women tried to combine paid work and family, but this was difficult to achieve. One woman, Ethel Puffer Howes, campaigned to make life easier for working wives and mothers. In 1925, she founded the Institute for the Coordination of Women's Interests at Smith College in Northampton, Massachusetts. This offered a variety of services, such as day care for children, intended to help

> ## DESIRABLE THINGS
>
> *"Suppose all women of ability could plan for love and children and for the joy of the working! . . . Then women would . . . have all the really desirable things."*
>
> In 1922, psychologist Ethel Puffer Howes described her vision for combining work with family life

12

married women combine work both inside and outside of the home. It set an example for similar organizations in the United States.

SERIOUS PROBLEMS

Women in poor communities faced serious problems. Most American cities and towns had run-down slums where families lived in cramped, unhealthy, and dangerous conditions. The women in these families suffered appallingly, struggling to support large numbers of children, with husbands who were often drunk and abusive.

In the early years of the 20th century, a group of progressive women set up movements to address these social problems, and their efforts continued in the 1920s and 1930s, especially through the work of Margaret Sanger, Dorothy Day, and Grace Abbott.

BIRTH CONTROL

Margaret Sanger and her supporters saw birth control as a way of helping women in poverty by allowing them to have smaller families. They claimed that birth control offered more freedom to women of all classes. Starting in 1916, Sanger opened a series of birth-control clinics, offering contraceptive devices and advice for women. In 1921, she organized the First American Birth Control Conference in New

WOMEN OF COURAGE AND CONVICTION

DOROTHY DAY (1897–1980)

Dorothy Day worked as a journalist and campaigner for social reform. In 1927 she converted to the Catholic faith and became a leading figure in the Catholic Worker Movement, committed to non-violence, justice, and hospitality to those in need. Day was editor of the *Catholic Worker*, a monthly newspaper that aimed to raise awareness of the problems of the poor. She also helped to establish a "house of hospitality" in the slums of New York and a series of farms where homeless people could live and work together.

Below: Many families struggled to survive in dreadful conditions. This photo was taken in 1937 in the slums of Washington, D.C.

Right: Children in city slums grew up in buildings that were filthy, crowded, and dangerous. While the children played outside, their mothers slaved to keep their families clean and fed.

York City. This led to the founding of the American Birth Control League, with the aim of educating all sectors of the public and setting up clinics across the United States.

CHILD WELFARE

The health of children from poor families was a major cause for concern among progressive reformers, such as Grace Abbott. In particular, the reformers were concerned about the high number of babies who died in their first year of life. In 1921, the U.S. Children's Bureau, which had been set up in 1912, found that infant and maternal mortality rates in the United States were among the highest of any developed nation. These findings led to the passing of the Sheppard-Towner Maternity and Infancy Protection Act of 1921, which provided funding for state agencies to set up public clinics offering prenatal and early childhood care. The Act had a major impact, improving the health of thousands of pregnant women and young children, but government funding came to an end in 1929. Despite the efforts of campaigners, child welfare measures were not reintroduced until 1935, when the government launched a program of aid to dependent children as part of the New Deal.

TEMPERANCE AND PROHIBITION

Another major social problem in the United States was the excessive consumption of alcohol. Since the 1870s, members of the temperance movement, including many determined women, had campaigned tirelessly for a total ban on alcohol, claiming it was the cause of a range of social problems such as domestic violence, poverty, and crime. In 1920, the temperance campaigners achieved their aim when the government passed the Prohibition Act, banning the sale, manufacture, and transportation of alcohol.

THE PROHIBITION ERA

Following the passing of the Prohibition Act, breweries, distilleries, and bars were shut down across the United States. Over 1,500 federal Prohibition agents were given the job of enforcing the law, but this proved an almost impossible task. Smugglers, known as bootleggers, managed to import vast quantities of alcohol over the U.S. border with Canada. Spirits and beer were made illegally, and speakeasies (illegal bars) sprang up in American cities. The most famous bootlegger was mobster Al Capone, whose gang was based in Chicago. Some women also became involved in smuggling, including, allegedly, movie star Clara Bow.

Prohibition failed to bring the improvements in social welfare that the temperance campaigners had hoped for. It was also very unpopular with the general public, especially during the years of the Great Depression. Eventually, in December 1933, the government passed a law to repeal (cancel) the Prohibition Act.

HOMELESS WOMEN

The Great Depression caused widespread unemployment and homelessness, and many people ended up living in rough situations. A large number of these homeless people were women. Organizations such as the YWCA (the Young Women's Christian

♥ *WOMEN OF COURAGE AND CONVICTION*

GRACE ABBOTT (1878–1939)

Grace Abbot was a social worker, a campaigner for child welfare, and an active member of the Immigrants' Protective League and the Women's Trade Union League. She served in the child labor division of the U.S. Children's Bureau, investigating working conditions in shipbuilding plants and factories across the United States. From 1934 until her death in 1939, Abbott was closely involved in the running of the Social Security Administration program (part of the New Deal), concentrating on child welfare.

Below: Welfare activist Grace Abbot never married and devoted her life to her social campaigns.

HUNGRY AND LONELY PEOPLE

"*I am thirty years old as I write this and have been a hobo for fifteen years, a sister of the road—one of that strange and motley sorority [sisterhood] which has increased its membership so greatly since the depression. . . . All my life I have lived with hungry and lonely people.*"

An extract from *Sister of the Road: The Autobiography of Boxcar Bertha* (1937)

Association, which had been founded in the 1850s) tried to provide accommodations and food for the large homeless population, but it was an impossible task.

The YWCA estimated that there were around 145,000 homeless females in America in the early 1930s. The wretched way of life of these women was brought to the public's attention in 1937 by a book called *Sister of the Road: The Autobiography of Boxcar Bertha*. Written by Ben Reitman, a doctor in Chicago, the book is loosely based on the real-life experiences of Bertha Thompson, a woman

Below: A migrant cotton-picking family from Texas, living in a trailer in an open field with no sanitation or fresh water.

who was forced through poverty to become a hobo, living in the boxcars of trains, traveling across the United States.

A LAWLESS TIME

The desperate circumstances of the Great Depression led to a wave of lawbreaking since some people were forced to steal simply to stay alive. Desperate individuals committed many small thefts, but there were also serious crimes carried out by armed gangs who moved from town to town, breaking into stores, gas stations, and banks.

The most famous outlaws of the period were Bonnie Parker and Clyde Barrow, who belonged to a criminal gang that traveled through Texas and nearby states. Members of the gang are believed to have killed at least nine police officers and several civilians.

REBUILDING LIVES

In 1933, newly elected President Roosevelt began to introduce a range of measures designed to help the American people recover from the effects of the Great Depression. The New Deal was an ongoing policy that included social relief programs, such as the Social Security Act, which gave financial support to the unemployed, and resettlement projects, which provided new homes for the homeless.

Roosevelt also introduced some large-scale projects in farming and construction as a way of boosting employment; some of these projects created work opportunities for women. The New Deal helped to stimulate a gradual economic recovery in the United States, but many American families still faced extreme hardship in the closing years of the 1930s.

Right: Bonnie Parker posing in front of the gang's getaway car. The 1967 movie *Bonnie and Clyde*, starring Faye Dunaway and Warren Beatty, made her famous.

▶ *BREAKTHROUGH BIOGRAPHY*

BONNIE PARKER (1910–34)

Bonnie Parker grew up in poverty in Texas. She married at age sixteen, but her marriage lasted only three years. In 1930, she met and fell in love with Clyde Barrow and joined his gang. From 1932 until her death two years later at age twenty-three, she took part in many armed robberies, although she claimed never to have fired a gun. In 1934, Bonnie and Clyde were ambushed and shot dead by six policemen.

CHAPTER 3

WOMEN AT WORK

D URING THE TWO DECADES FROM 1920 TO 1940, the number of American women working outside the home increased slightly. In 1920, women made up 23.6 percent of the labor force; by 1940, this percentage had risen to 25.4. Some advances were made in working women's rights, but during the Great Depression, many female workers lost their jobs or were forced to accept severe cuts in pay. Despite the economic difficulties of the period, some outstanding businesswomen achieved great commercial success.

LOW PAY AND LONG HOURS

Working women were paid substantially less than men, and the Great Depression caused female pay to fall even more. Factory owners deliberately hired women rather than men because they could get away with paying them much less. Most women also worked very long hours. In the 1930s, over half of all employed women worked more than fifty hours a week. This situation was especially hard on working mothers, who had to leave their children alone at home.

> ### PINNED TOGETHER
>
> "A woman's so-called pin money is often the family coupling pin, the only means of holding the family together and making ends meet."
>
> Women's Bureau president Mary Anderson

Left: Women in factories worked long hours at tiring and boring tasks. This factory worker is sorting through candy on a conveyor belt.

Right: The cover of a monthly magazine for blue-collar workers features an illustration of union organizer Ella Mae Wiggins.

The misery of the female worker, forced to work long hours away from her children and still unable to pay for all their needs, is powerfully expressed in the poems of Ella Mae Wiggins, a mill worker, ballad writer, and campaigner for better working conditions for women.

"PIN MONEY" OR FAMILY SUPPORT?

Campaigners for higher pay for women faced an uphill struggle, especially when confronted with the view that women's wages were not essential to a family's income. In 1933, a report compiled for President Herbert Hoover on recent social trends claimed that women worked for "pin money," in other words, for treats and not in order to support themselves or their families. The Women's Bureau produced evidence that this was not the case, drawing on studies that showed that 90 percent of employed women used their wages to support their families. The bureau also revealed that 25 percent of employed women were primary wage earners in a family unit and 66 percent of single employed women contributed their wages toward supporting a household.

PROTECTION OR EQUAL PAY?

One of the problems facing campaigners for equal pay was the idea that women should be allowed "protected" working conditions, such as shorter hours or less demanding physical work than men. This problem was highlighted in 1923 in the court case of *Adkins v. the Children's Hospital*. In this case, two women sought compensation because their employers had dismissed them rather than increase their pay to the minimum wage established by state law. The judge ruled against the women's right to a minimum wage and in favor of the principle of special protection, stating that the women had the right to negotiate the terms of their employment. This judgment divided campaigners for working women's rights. Some activists saw the *Adkins* decision as a step toward better treatment and respect for women. Others saw it as a step backward, condemning women to lives of low wages and poverty.

♥ WOMEN OF COURAGE AND CONVICTION

ELLA MAE WIGGINS (1900–29)

Ella Mae Wiggins lived in Gaston County, North Carolina, where she was a spinner at the local mill. She had nine children, but four of them died in an outbreak of whooping cough. Wiggins became a labor union organizer, recruiting black workers as well as white. She also composed ballads about the harsh conditions of the mill worker's life. At the age of twenty-eight, she was ambushed and shot dead by state troopers on her way to a labor union meeting.

Above: Female strikers try to disarm a National Guard soldier during the Gastonia strike of 1929. The factory owners had called in the soldiers to break up the strike, with orders to use violence if necessary.

TEXTILE WORKERS' STRIKES

A large proportion of women worked in textile mills and clothing factories, where they had to cope with poor conditions, punishing hours, and very low pay. In the 1920s, their work became even harder as factory owners demanded ever-higher rates of productivity. Eventually, the workers could not stand it any longer and withdrew their labor in a wave of strikes that broke out in the late 1920s and early 1930s.

One of the first strikes took place in 1929 at a rayon factory in Elizabethton, Tennessee, when Margaret Bowen led a walkout of

523 women operatives. The strike finally ended when the factory owner called in armed troops to deal with the women, who had to agree to the owner's terms and conditions.

THE GASTONIA STRIKE

Before the Elizabethton strike ended, thousands of textile workers had walked out of factories in Marion and Gastonia, North Carolina, and other clothing mills across the southern states. Few of the strikes were successful, however, and in several cases the factory owners called in the state troops. The most extreme use of force occurred in Gastonia, where soldiers ambushed and killed Ella Mae Wiggins.

ROSE PESOTTA AND THE LOS ANGELES DRESSMAKERS' STRIKE

In October 1933, a city-wide strike of garment workers broke out in Los Angeles. Most of the workers were Mexican-American women, who spoke little English and were desperate for work, and their employers exploited them cruelly. Early in 1933, the International

> ### SCRATCHING A LIVING
>
> "We leave our homes in the morning,
> We kiss our children good-bye,
> While we slave for the bosses,
> Our children scream and cry.
>
> And when we draw our money,
> Our grocery bills to pay,
> Not a cent to spend for clothing,
> Not a cent to lay away."
>
> Verses from *A Mill Mother's Lament,* a workers' protest ballad written by Ella Mae Wiggins

WOMEN OF COURAGE AND CONVICTION

ROSE PESOTTA (1896–1965)

Rose Pesotta was born in Ukraine but emigrated to the United States at age seventeen. She worked in a clothing factory in New York and soon became an active member of the International Ladies' Garment Workers' Union (ILGWU). Pesotta worked tirelessly to help educate women workers about their rights. In 1933, she helped organize the Los Angeles dressmakers' strike, and her success led to her appointment as vice president of the ILGWU. In 1937, she helped to establish unions for garment workers in Montreal, Canada.

Left: As a dressmaker, Rose Pesotta had witnessed firsthand the way women were treated in the garment industry.

TURNING POINT

THE FOUNDING OF THE DOMESTIC WORKERS' UNION

In 1934, Dora Jones, an African-American woman, founded the Domestic Workers' Union in New York to give support to cleaners, maids, and other domestic servants. Until the union was formed, domestic workers had no way of protesting their working conditions. In particular, African Americans, who made up a large proportion of domestic workers, were sometimes treated extremely badly. The union allowed domestic workers to join together to demand better treatment and pay.

Ladies' Garment Workers' Union (ILGWU) sent labor activist Rose Pesotta from New York to support the workers of Los Angeles. Pesotta made use of bilingual radio and newspaper campaigns to organize the women into a labor union and played a leading role in their strike. The Los Angeles dressmakers' strike lasted for a month and involved roughly 2,000 women from eighty factories. After the strike, conditions in the city's garment industry gradually improved.

BLACK AND WHITE UNITE

In 1933, Connie Smith led a successful strike of 900 black women working in seven pecan-nut factories in St. Louis, Missouri. Smith demanded higher pay, better working conditions, and the removal of differences in pay between black and white women workers. The factories' owner tried to divide the workers, offering white women an increase in wages if they returned to work. In answer to this, 1,500 women marched in protest to the city hall, forcing the factory owner to agree to the women's demands. Wages were increased, conditions improved, and white and black women were granted equal pay.

Below: On February 5, 1937, a group of wives and mothers demonstrate their support for the striking male workers at the General Motors Plant in Flint, Michigan, while on the right a man and woman embrace.

HELPING MALE STRIKERS

In addition to fighting for the rights of female workers, some women gave their support to men in their struggles for better pay and conditions. During a sit-down strike at General Motors in Flint, Michigan, twenty-three-year-old Genora Johnson Dollinger, who was married to one of the strikers, decided that the men needed some help. Within a few days of the start of the strike, Dollinger had mobilized a branch of the Women's Emergency Brigade to bring in food and supplies to the striking workers inside the factory. She also organized support for the families of the strikers. Brigade members armed themselves with clubs to defend the strikers from police attacks and broke factory windows when tear gas was used on the men inside the plant. With the support of the Women's Brigade, the strike continued for forty-four days and resulted in victory for the strikers when the factory owners were forced to sign a contract with the union. Dollinger was nicknamed "the Joan of Arc of Labor" for her role in the strike.

SHOP ASSISTANTS SIT DOWN

During the period 1920 to 1940, many women found employment in the numerous shops and stores that were opening up in American towns and cities. Shop work was seen as a pleasant job, but sales staff were poorly paid. In 1937, male and female workers at several dime stores in

WOMEN CRUSADERS

"Greetings and congratulations to . . . the members of the Women's Emergency Brigade. The automobile workers of Flint and America owe you a debt of gratitude for the part you played in the winning of The Big Strike and in building our International Union. You are truly crusaders in this new American Labor Movement, and your fighting spirit an inspiration to all workers!"

Roy Reuther, Flint strike organizer, 1937

Below: Dime-store girls worked very long hours. They were on their feet all day and were expected to be always pleasant, cheerful, and helpful. The girl in this photo is showing the strain, however!

> **BREAKTHROUGH BIOGRAPHY**

MARGARET FOGARTY RUDKIN (1897–1976)

Margaret Fogarty Rudkin was the wife of a wealthy banker. She lived in a farmhouse in Connecticut called Pepperidge Farm. When her youngest son became ill with asthma, her doctor recommended healthy, home-cooked food. Rudkin started baking bread, using her Irish grandmother's recipes, and soon set up a small bakery to sell her loaves. By 1940, she was receiving orders from all over the United States. During the next ten years, the Pepperidge Farm brand grew very fast, becoming an international food company.

Right: Margaret Rudkin, founder of the Pepperidge Farm bakery.

New York held a sit-down strike, locking themselves inside their stores and sleeping behind the counters at night. Their protest was successful, and they won a pay increase.

WOMEN IN BUSINESS

Some women achieved great commercial success in the 1920s and 1930s. In the early 1920s, Lila Acheson Wallace co-founded *Reader's Digest* magazine, while Ida Kaganovich Rosenthal opened her first factory for Maidenform bras. By the end of the 1930s, both women were multi-millionaires.

Three American women built up thriving food companies in this period. Ruth Graves Wakefield invented the Toll House chocolate chip cookie and turned it into a winning brand, while Margaret Fogarty Rudkin founded the highly successful Pepperidge Farm Company.

In 1927, Gretchen Schoenleber became president of her family's Ambrosia Chocolate Company. Under her direction, the company survived the Wall Street Crash, and the following year she organized the building of a four-story addition to the Ambrosia factory.

NEW CAREERS

In the second two decades of the 20th century, women began to make their mark in careers formerly dominated by men. A growing number of women became doctors, lawyers, and architects, and in 1932, Ruth Nichols became the first woman to be hired as a pilot for commercial passenger flights.

WORK IN THE DEPRESSION YEARS

Although some women managed to pursue rewarding careers, the 1930s were not good years for female workers. Faced with the problems of widespread unemployment, the government decided to offer more families the chance of work. In 1933, the National Industrial Recovery Act made it illegal for more than one family member to hold a government position. This meant that many women lost their jobs.

The work creation programs of the New Deal resulted in some new jobs for women, although opportunities were mainly restricted to widows or wives of disabled men. While men were often trained in new work skills, women were generally given unskilled tasks, such as sewing clothes for the poor, serving lunches to schoolchildren, and helping older people. Each state was responsible for its own work programs, so local prejudices sometimes came into play. In the South, black women were frequently given hard and dangerous manual tasks, such as clearing land, working in dumps and garbage incinerators, and hoeing tobacco fields.

Right: In 1936, a group of women in Minneapolis, Minnesota, take part in a New Deal sewing project organized by the Works Progress Administration.

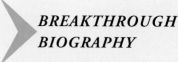

BREAKTHROUGH BIOGRAPHY

JULIA MORGAN (1872–1957)

Julia Morgan was a leading architect at a time when there were almost no women practicing architecture. She studied civil engineering at the University of California, Berkeley, and architecture in Paris, France. In 1904, she set up an architectural practice in San Francisco. During her long career, Morgan designed over 700 buildings and specialized in schools and colleges for girls. She is best known for her work on Hearst Castle, an extravagant and ornate mansion built for newspaper tycoon William Randolph Hearst in San Simeon, California.

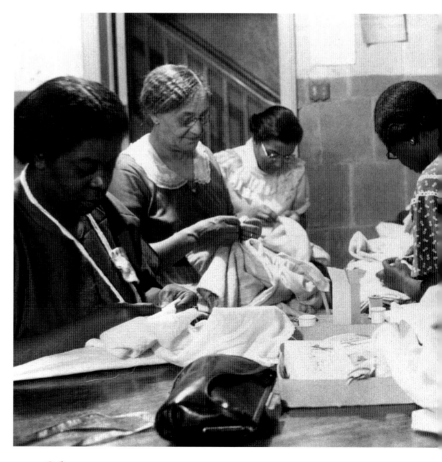

CHAPTER 4

EDUCATION, SCIENCE, AND POLITICS

B Y THE 1920S, ALL GIRLS LIVING IN THE UNITED STATES had the chance to get a basic education. Every state required children to attend an elementary school, and most towns had public high schools for boys and girls. Girls from privileged backgrounds attended private schools, and it was common for daughters as well as sons to study at a college or university. Meanwhile, on the political front, women joined various pressure groups to fight for fair treatment between the sexes.

Above: At college in the 1920s and 1930s, girls were encouraged to acquire a wide range of skills. These students from Indiana are practicing archery.

SCIENCE AND MEDICINE

Some remarkable women worked in the fields of science and medicine. Katharine Blodgett was a physicist employed by the General Electric Company, where she invented low-reflection "invisible" glass. Gerty Theresa Cori was part of a medical research team awarded a Nobel

Prize for its work on the digestive system, and Hattie Alexander did pioneering research in the field of treating infections with drugs.

MARGARET MEAD, ANTHROPOLOGIST

Margaret Mead was a courageous and groundbreaking scholar who helped to popularize the academic discipline of anthropology. In particular, she reported on attitudes toward sex in South Pacific traditional cultures and championed a more relaxed approach to sexual behavior in Western life.

Mead's most famous work was *Coming of Age in Samoa*, a study of Samoan girls between the ages of nine and twenty. One of Mead's aims in the book was to compare the experience of adolescents in Samoa with that of Western teenagers. She concluded that girls in Samoa experienced a smooth transition from childhood to adulthood and noted that their adolescence was not marked by the distress, anxiety, and confusion seen in American teenagers.

STUDYING WOMEN'S HISTORY

By the 1920s, there was growing interest in the history of women. Some female scholars felt that this area of research was not taken seriously by male historians, who focused instead on the achievements of men. In 1926, a group of scholars met in Berkshire, Massachusetts, and set up the Berkshire Conference on the History of

BREAKTHROUGH BIOGRAPHY

HATTIE ALEXANDER (1901–68)

Hattie Alexander worked in the public health system before starting to train as a doctor. She received her doctoral degree in 1930, at age twenty-nine, and two years later became an instructor and researcher in the Department of Pediatrics at Columbia University in New York. Alexander spent the rest of her career at Columbia, conducting research into infections affecting babies and children. She helped to develop drugs to treat a form of childhood influenza and was one of the first scientists to research the problem of resistance to antibiotic drugs. Alexander received many awards in recognition of her outstanding contributions to medical science.

TURNING POINT

ATTITUDES TO SEX

In 1928, anthropologist Margaret Mead published *Coming of Age in Samoa*. The book outraged some people because it challenged conventional Western attitudes toward sex before marriage. The publication of *Coming of Age in Samoa* was later seen as one of the first steps toward the sexual revolution that took place in the 1960s.

Left: Through her groundbreaking books, scientist Margaret Mead brought the study of cultural anthropology to a wide audience.

STUMBLING BLOCKS

"[Our ambition is] to remove the remaining legal discriminations against women in the codes and constitutions of the several states in order that the feet of coming women may find these stumbling blocks removed."

From a rousing speech by Carrie Chapman Catt, outlining the aims of the National League of Women Voters

Women. Their aim was to hold regular conferences to discuss new findings in women's history. The Berkshire conferences are still held today and play a vital role in promoting the study of women's history.

CAMPAIGNING WOMEN

In August 1920, the 19th Amendment to the Constitution of the United States was passed, granting women in all states the right to vote. After nearly a century of campaigning, the women's suffrage movement had finally achieved its aim. However, many suffragists felt there was still much work to be done to achieve fair treatment for women.

Women worked within different pressure groups to achieve their aims. Some of the leading women's groups in the period were the National Woman's Party (NWP), led by Alice Paul; the National Association of Colored Women, led by Mary McLeod Bethune; and the National League of Women Voters (NLWV), founded by Carrie Chapman Catt.

THE NATIONAL LEAGUE OF WOMEN VOTERS

The NLWV was established in 1920, six months before the 19th Amendment was passed. Its founders looked forward to the period after

Below: Women unfurl a banner on the steps leading up to the headquarters of the National League of Women Voters in Washington, D.C.

WOMEN OF COURAGE AND CONVICTION

ALICE PAUL
(1885–1977)

Alice Paul was brought up as a Quaker in New Jersey and studied political science in the United States and Britain. From 1913 on, she led the National Woman's Party in a determined campaign for women's suffrage. As a campaigner, Paul took a more radical stand than the other suffrage leaders, using a range of militant methods, including silent protests and hunger strikes. After women had gained the vote, Paul moved on to her next objective: equal rights for women. In 1923, she proposed the Equal Rights Amendment (ERA) to Congress, but she did not succeed in getting it passed.

Left: Following the success of her radical campaign for women's suffrage, Alice Paul was determined to achieve equal rights for women.

women had gained the vote, when they could begin to play a more active role in politics, and made plans for their campaign of action.

The NLWV aimed to remove any legal discrimination against women and to educate women about their rights. Members of the League were committed to scrutinizing the government's social policies to make sure that they were truly fair. The League rejected the idea of forming a "woman's party." Instead, it encouraged its members to work inside the existing political parties.

THE CABLE ACT
In the 1920s, members of the NLWV campaigned for the passage of two government acts that would have an impact on women's lives. One was

Above: The National Woman's Party was one of the groups that supported equal rights for women. Members of the NWP are shown here at a meeting in 1922.

ORDINARY EQUALITY

"I never doubted that equal rights was the right direction. Most reforms, most problems are complicated. But to me there is nothing complicated about ordinary equality."

Alice Paul, interviewed in 1972 about her role in the suffrage campaign

the Sheppard-Towner Maternity Act of 1921, which would provide support for mothers and children. The other was the Cable Act. Until the Cable Act was passed, women who married foreigners had to give up their U.S. citizenship and adopt the citizenship of their husband's country. This was unjust since American men with foreign wives did not lose their rights as American citizens. The Cable Act, which was passed in 1922, removed this discrimination against women and allowed the wives of foreigners to keep their citizenship.

EQUAL RIGHTS FOR WOMEN?

In 1923, Alice Paul proposed a new amendment to the United States Constitution. Known as the Equal Rights Amendment, it simply stated, "Men and women shall have equal rights throughout the United States and every place subject to its jurisdiction."

Paul's proposal split the women's movement in two. One of the groups in favor of the ERA was the National Association of Colored Women, but the League of Women Voters was opposed to it. The supporters said that women should have equal rights with men in all areas of life. However, Paul's opponents believed that the amendment would make life harder for many women. They were concerned that if the ERA was passed, the laws protecting women at work would have to be canceled. Without these labor protection laws, employers could insist that female employees work night shifts and handle heavy and dangerous machinery alongside male employees.

Congress did not accept Alice Paul's amendment in 1923. After its defeat, the ERA was presented to Congress almost every year, but each time it was rejected. Even today, there is still no statement in the U.S. Constitution that women should have equal rights with men.

WORKING FOR PEACE

Some women put their energies into a determined attempt to prevent any future wars. American women had campaigned for peace for centuries, but the appalling casualties suffered in World War I gave a new urgency to the peace movement in the 1920s. In 1921, Caroline Lexow Babcock and Elinor Byrns organized the Women's Peace Union (WPU) with the aim of putting pressure on the government to outlaw war entirely.

To achieve their ambitious aim, members of the WPU used non-violent methods such as public meetings and letter-writing campaigns. They also employed the tactic of praising women for their peaceful instincts and criticizing men for their aggressive behavior. WPU members believed it was the duty of women to save men from their stupidity and so put an end to all wars.

The greatest achievement of the women's peace movement came in 1928, when sixty-two nations, led by the United States and France, signed the Kellogg–Briand Pact. This was an agreement by which the signatories agreed to renounce war as a way of advancing national ambitions

WOMEN OF COURAGE AND CONVICTION

CAROLINE LEXOW BABCOCK (1892–1981)

Caroline Lexow Babcock grew up in South Nyack, New York. Apart from her work as co-founder and leader of the Women's Peace Union, she played an active part in the struggle for women's suffrage and campaigned for the abolition of capital punishment. Babcock was a member of the National Woman's Party and a passionate supporter of Alice Paul's attempts to achieve equal rights for women.

Below: Students played a significant role in the women's peace movement, taking part in parades and demonstrations. This photograph shows a group of students from Vassar College in New York State. Around 1,000 Vassar students took part in peace campaigns.

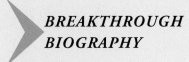

BREAKTHROUGH BIOGRAPHY

MINNIE FISHER CUNNINGHAM (1882–1964)

Minnie Fisher Cunningham (known as Minnie Fish) grew up in Texas and trained as a pharmacist. She was a passionate campaigner for suffrage and a founding leader of the National League of Women Voters. In 1928, she was unsuccessful in her attempt to be elected as a senator. Nevertheless, she held important posts in Texas. From 1932 to 1944, she ran major state agencies, providing support for farmers.

TURNING POINT

FIRST BLACK WOMAN IN GOVERNMENT

In 1936, President Roosevelt appointed African American Mary McLeod Bethune as director of Negro Affairs in the National Youth Administration project. Bethune was the first black woman to be given a major government appointment and act as adviser to a U.S. president.

Right: Nellie Tayloe Ross was governor of Wyoming from 1925 to 1927 and director of the U.S. Mint from 1933 to 1953. She was a staunch supporter of Prohibition in the 1920s.

or settling international arguments. However, by the late 1930s, many people believed that war with Adolf Hitler's Germany was inevitable, and the WPU lost most of its support.

WOMEN IN GOVERNMENT

Not long after they gained the right to vote, women began to enter the world of politics. In 1925, Nellie Tayloe Ross became the first woman to serve as a state governor after her husband, the governor of Wyoming, died in office. His sudden death prompted the Democratic Party to nominate Nellie to run for governor in a special election the following month. In 1926, Nellie ran for a second term of office but was defeated. However, in 1933, President Roosevelt appointed her as the first female director of the U.S. Mint, where she served five full terms until her retirement in 1953.

In 1925, Miriam Wallace Ferguson ran for the office of governor of Texas after her husband lost his position because of improper conduct.

She served as state governor until 1927 and was re-elected for a second term in 1933.

THE FIRST ELECTED WOMAN SENATOR

Another woman who took over her husband's position was Hattie Caraway. When her husband died in 1931, she was automatically given his place in the Senate as a way of holding on to the seat until the next election. However, when the election came, she surprised her local party by declaring that she would run for the Senate in her own right. Caraway won her seat in 1932, becoming the first elected female senator. She was a senator until 1945, taking a special interest in relief for farmers, flood control, and benefits for army veterans.

FRANCES PERKINS, SECRETARY OF LABOR

The most outstanding female politician of the 1930s was Frances Perkins. As a young woman, she campaigned for workers' rights and in 1918 became the first female member of the New York State Industrial Commission. In 1929, the newly elected governor of New York, Franklin D. Roosevelt, appointed Perkins as the state industrial commissioner. Following Roosevelt's election as president, Perkins was given the post of secretary of labor, becoming the first woman to hold a cabinet position in the U.S. government.

Below: Politician Frances Perkins greets a group of workers in her role as secretary of labor.

Perkins was secretary of labor from 1933 to 1945. During her twelve-year term of office, she ran work creation schemes as part of Roosevelt's New Deal. She established unemployment benefits and welfare for the poorest Americans and introduced laws to reduce workplace accidents and restrict child labor. She also established the first minimum wage and overtime laws for American workers and defined the standard forty-hour workweek.

CHAPTER 5

SPORTS, DANCE, AND FILM

AS A LEGACY OF THE ROARING TWENTIES, WOMEN became much more active than they had been in previous generations. This new sense of freedom continued into the 1930s and provided in some ways an antidote to the troubles of that period. Female athletes competed in national and international events. Female dancers pioneered new forms of dance, and the rapid growth of the movie industry made American actresses into international stars.

Below: Tennis star Helen Wills has been described as the first American-born woman to achieve international celebrity as an athlete.

TENNIS

By the 1920s, American women were competing in tennis championships at home and abroad. In 1923, Helen Wills won the women's singles title at the U.S. championships. The next year, she won two gold medals (for singles and doubles) at the Paris Olympics. This marked the start of a brilliant career in which she won eighteen singles and nine doubles titles in competitions in the United States, Britain, and France.

Two more tennis champions emerged in the 1930s. African-American player Ora Washington won the American Tennis Association's singles title eight times. Elizabeth Ryan achieved an all-time record by winning nineteen doubles titles at the British championships held at Wimbledon.

SWIMMING

The United States produced several swimming champions in the years 1920 to 1940. In 1922,

Above: Gertrude Ederle is slathered in goose fat before her plunge into the English Channel. Her swim took 14 hours, 31 minutes, shaving almost two hours off the previous record held by a man.

Sybil Bauer broke both the men's and women's world records in the 440-yard backstroke event, and within two years she had set twenty-one records for women. In 1932, Helene Madison won three gold medals in freestyle at the 1932 Summer Olympic Games and went on to set seventeen world records in her career.

Eleanor Holm and Esther Williams were both champion swimmers who went on to pursue careers in movies. The most famous woman swimmer of the period was Gertrude Ederle. In addition to taking part in competitions, she was the first woman to swim across the English Channel, a feat she achieved in 1926.

ATHLETICS

In 1922, the Amateur Athletic Union (AAU) added women's track-and-field events to their list of recognized sports. Female athletes began to compete in a range of events, including running, hurdling, throwing the

> ## BREAKTHROUGH BIOGRAPHY
>
> ### GERTRUDE EDERLE (1905–2003)
>
> Gertrude Ederle was the daughter of a butcher and grew up in New York. She began to train as a competitive swimmer at age thirteen and set more amateur records than any other woman in the world. In 1924, she won an Olympic gold medal, and in 1926, at age nineteen, she swam the English Channel, a distance of approximately twenty-one miles. In 1933, she damaged her spine and stopped competitive swimming; she also became increasingly deaf. Ederle never married and spent much of her adult life teaching swimming to deaf children.

> ## BREAKTHROUGH BIOGRAPHY
>
> ### ORA WASHINGTON (1898–1971)
>
> Ora Washington was a tennis and basketball champion who grew up in Philadelphia. She won the American Tennis Association's national singles title eight times between 1929 and 1937 and was also a champion basketball player. Washington played basketball for the Philadelphia Tribunes from 1932 to 1942 and was the team's leading scorer and coach. She retired from tennis in the mid-1940s after Helen Wills refused to play with her. For the rest of her life, she worked as a housekeeper.

Above: Babe Didrikson, second from the right, races to Olympic victory as winner of the women's 80-meter hurdles in Los Angeles in 1932.

AIMING HIGH

"Before I was in my teens, I knew exactly what I wanted to be: I wanted to be the best athlete who ever lived."

Babe Didrikson Zaharias

javelin, and high and long jump. Six years later, in 1928, female track-and-field athletes took part in the Olympic Games for the first time.

In the 1932 Olympics, one female athlete stood out from all the others. Mildred Didrikson, nicknamed "Babe" (who later used her married name of Zaharias), won two gold medals and one silver medal. In the trials held before the Olympics, she competed in eight out of ten track-and-field events, winning five and tying for first place in a sixth. During these trials, she set five world records in a single afternoon.

AN ALL-ROUND ATHLETE

Babe Didrikson Zaharias competed successfully in a remarkable number of sports. In addition to her triumphs in track-and-field at the Olympics, she achieved great success in basketball and golf. In 1933, she led her basketball team, the Golden Cyclones, to the finals of the national championships. Later she toured with her own team, known as "Babe Didrikson's All-Americans basketball team." In 1935, Babe began to play golf and went on to become the leading female American player of the 1940s, winning thirty-one tournaments. She also played baseball and softball and was an expert diver and roller skater.

BASEBALL

Baseball was very popular among young women in the 1920s, and many American cities had a female baseball team. Team members often started playing very young; Edith Houghton was just ten years old when she became the star of the Philadelphia Bobbies.

Lizzie Murphy and Jackie Mitchell were such skilled players that they were recruited to play in teams alongside men. Murphy became the only female member of the Boston All-Stars and attracted large crowds, who came mostly to see her play. Jackie Mitchell played for the Chattanooga Lookouts. In 1931, her team played the New York Yankees, and the seventeen-year-old managed to strike out two of the Yankees' greatest hitters. A few days after the game, the U.S. baseball commissioner canceled Murphy's contract with her team, claiming that baseball was "too strenuous" for women. In 1933, the U.S. Women's Lacrosse and Amateur Softball Associations organized their first tournaments. The introduction of softball meant women's baseball began to be phased out. By 1935 many female baseball teams had been disbanded.

DANCING DUOS

The 1920s were a great time for dancing, and young men and women performed energetic routines to jazz and ragtime tunes. In the years leading up to World War I, Irene and Vernon Castle had introduced ragtime numbers to New York, and Irene continued

---

Right: Jackie Mitchell shot to fame when she managed to strike out male baseball legend Babe Ruth.

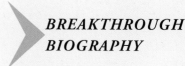

BREAKTHROUGH BIOGRAPHY

LIZZIE MURPHY (1894–1964)

Lizzie Murphy grew up on Rhode Island. She started her baseball career at age fifteen, playing for amateur teams before signing with the Providence Independents. From there, she moved to the Boston All-Stars, a semi-professional team. In 1922, she was picked to play for the Boston Red Sox in a charity game, becoming the first woman to play for a major-league team, and in 1928 she played in a National League All-Star game. Murphy retired in 1935 after seventeen years of playing professional baseball.

GINGER ROGERS (1911–95)

Ginger Rogers grew up in Missouri and Texas. As a teenager, she joined a traveling vaudeville show. At the age of eighteen, she got a part in a Broadway show, where she was spotted by George and Ira Gershwin, who chose her to star in their new musical, *Girl Crazy*. This made Rogers an instant star, and in 1930 she signed a contract with a movie company. Rogers's film breakthrough came in 1933 with *42nd Street*, and in the same year she made her first movie with Fred Astaire. Her partnership with Astaire ended in 1939, but she went on to enjoy a successful acting career.

Right: Fred Astaire and Ginger Rogers earned international fame as dancing partners. One of the couple's most famous numbers was "Let's Face the Music and Dance."

to appear in movies and stage shows in the 1920s, following Vernon's death in the war. Another great dancing duo of the 1920s was Fred Astaire and his sister, Adele, but it was not until the 1930s that Fred found his ideal partner in Ginger Rogers. Rogers and Astaire made ten movies together, including *Top Hat* and *Swing Time*.

BREAKING FREE FROM BALLET

Some pioneering dancers broke away from classical ballet in the 1920s and 1930s. Isadora Duncan dressed in flowing robes and scarves and danced barefoot, illustrating themes from classical myths. Duncan spent most of her adult life in Europe, but her very individual style had an impact on dancers in the United States. Another pioneer of the period was Ruth St. Denis, who developed a style of dance based on mystical ideas with a strong oriental element. In 1938, she founded a dance program at Adelphi University in New York. The program, which continues today, played an important part in the development of modern dance.

MARTHA GRAHAM

The most outstanding dance pioneer of the period was Martha Graham. She was an astonishing performer and choreographer (creator of dances) who invented a new language of movement to express human emotions. Graham became a pupil of Ruth St. Dennis in 1911 and spent the next ten years working on her technique. By the 1920s, she was staging her own performances, and in 1926, she founded the Martha Graham Center of Contemporary Dance. Her real breakthrough came in 1936 with the performance of her war piece, *Chronicle*. She continued dancing until the 1960s and taught and inspired generations of leading dancers and choreographers.

TURNING POINT

THE POWER OF MODERN DANCE

In 1936, Martha Graham created *Chronicle*, a dance that reflected the spirit of the age. *Chronicle* was influenced by the Wall Street Crash, the Great Depression, and the Spanish Civil War and focused on the emotions of depression and isolation, expressed through the dancers' movements and costumes and through the stage set. This groundbreaking project demonstrated that dance could be used to express deep emotions and contemporary concerns and marked the beginning of a new era in contemporary dance.

Below: An early performance by the Martha Graham Dance Company. Graham's dancers stunned audiences with their simple costumes and dramatic movements.

VAUDEVILLE

Vaudeville acts, featuring a mixture of songs, dances, and comedy routines, were very popular in the early decades of the 20th century. Many vaudeville companies toured the United States, while a few were based on Broadway in New York City. The most famous company of the period, the Ziegfeld Follies, performed on Broadway from 1907 to 1931. In 1932, the company launched a radio program known as *The Ziegfeld Follies of the Air*, which ran for four years.

Below: Mae West was an American actress, playwright, and screenwriter. She was also a rebel who dared to behave in a deliberately sexy way.

Some of the "showgirls" who performed in vaudeville went on to become famous. Gypsy Rose Lee, Sophie Tucker, Fanny Brice, Josephine Baker, and Mae West all started their careers as showgirls but later moved into films.

THE SILENT SCREEN

The early 1920s were the golden years of silent movies. In cities and towns all over the United States, people flocked to newly built movie houses to see the latest productions, accompanied by a pianist, an organist, or even a full orchestra. Some leading male film stars of the silent era were comic actors Charlie Chaplin and Buster Keaton and romantic male lead Rudolph Valentino. Glamorous female stars included Gloria Swanson and sisters Dorothy and Lillian Gish.

THE "TALKIES"

The launch of *The Jazz Singer* in 1927 marked the arrival of the "talkies," and almost every film produced after 1930 had a sound track. The talkies required a different acting technique from silent films, and a new generation of stars emerged. American film stars of the 1930s included Katharine Hepburn, Mae West, Jean Harlow, and child actress Shirley Temple. Foreign stars Greta Garbo, from Sweden, and Marlene Dietrich, from Germany, arrived in Hollywood in the 1930s. They were greatly admired for their mystery and sophistication, and many American women copied their style.

Below: Comedian Fanny Brice was best known for her role as bratty toddler Baby Snooks. When she performed the role onstage, Brice dressed in a pink dress and short socks and had an enormous pink bow in her hair.

BREAKTHROUGH BIOGRAPHY

JOSEPHINE BAKER (1906–75)

Josephine Baker was the first African American to star in a major motion picture. She grew up in poverty in St. Louis, Missouri, and dropped out of school at age twelve. However, her street-corner dancing attracted the attention of a vaudeville show owner, and she started appearing onstage. In her late teens, she moved to New York, becoming one of the stars of Broadway vaudeville. In 1925, she moved to Paris, where she continued to perform as a dancer and entertainer. Baker spent most of the rest of her life in France. She starred in several French movies and also became a worldwide celebrity.

BREAKTHROUGH BIOGRAPHY

FANNY BRICE (1891–1951)

Fanny Brice came from a Hungarian-Jewish family and grew up in New York. In 1908, she dropped out of school to work in a vaudeville show, and two years later she joined the Ziegfeld Follies, where she was a major star from 1910 to the 1930s. Brice specialized in comic routines and was especially famous for her role as "Baby Snooks," a spoiled toddler. From 1936 until her death in 1951, she also performed the role of Baby Snooks on American radio. After Brice's death, a Broadway show and a movie, both called *Funny Girl*, were made about her life.

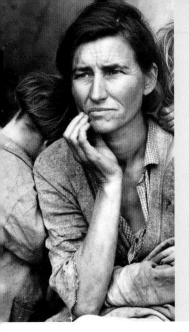

CHAPTER 6

THE ARTS

IN THE 1920S AND 1930S, WOMEN PLAYED AN ACTIVE role in the arts. There were prominent female playwrights, novelists, and poets. In the field of music, there were female composers, lyricists and performers. In art, women created beautiful paintings and sculptures; they also took extraordinary photographs. A significant contribution to the arts of this period was made by African Americans and other minority groups.

TURNING POINT

EXPERIMENTAL THEATER

Sophie Treadwell's play *Machinal* was first performed in New York in 1928, where it caused a sensation because of its daring theme, original structure, and extensive use of sound effects. The play was inspired by the case of Ruth Snyder, a young woman convicted of murder, and was written in nine scenes depicting different phases of her life. *Machinal* was seen as an outstanding example of experimental theater. It broke new ground in its portrayal of the emotional life of a disturbed young woman.

THEATER

Some women playwrights produced hard-hitting plays in this period. Clare Boothe Luce was a journalist and playwright who satirized wealthy New York society. Lillian Hellman, Sophie Treadwell, and Susan Glaspell all attacked social injustice and hypocrisy in their plays. Anita Loos wrote plays exposing corruption in wealthy society and at the same time pursued a career as a Hollywood screenwriter.

Right: A scene from Sophie Treadwell's *Machinal*. The play voices a powerful criticism of the modern, machine-driven world.

Playwright Hallie Flanagan was a pioneer of experimental theater in the 1920s. During the Great Depression, President Roosevelt recruited Flanagan to lead the Federal Theater Project as part of his policy of getting Americans back to work. In her work for the project, Flanagan created jobs for unemployed actors and brought cutting-edge theater to the American public. She established a children's theater and staged "Living Newspaper" dramas on topics of current interest. These productions toured the United States and were performed for millions of people.

CLASSICAL MUSIC

Between the years 1921 and 1937, women achieved some significant milestones in the field of classical music. In 1925, multi-talented pianist, composer, and conductor Ethel Leginska became the first woman to conduct a major American orchestra—the New York Symphony Orchestra, at Carnegie Hall. Two years later, she formed the Boston Women's Symphony Orchestra, which performed some of her works.

Female composer Amy Beach became well known for her choral works and romantic songs, while Florence Smith Price was the first African-American woman in the United States to be recognized as a composer of classical symphonies. In 1930, Ruth Crawford Seeger, who specialized in experimental "modernist" music, became the first woman to receive a Guggenheim Fellowship for musical composition.

MUSICALS

Women played an important role in the rise of the musical. In 1928, lyrics writer Dorothy Fields had her first big hit with the song "I Can't Give You Anything But Love," which was soon followed by "On the Sunny Side of the Street." She went on to work with

Right: Screenwriter, playwright, and author, Anita Loos proved that women could be as clever and funny as men.

BREAKTHROUGH BIOGRAPHY

ANITA LOOS (1888–1981)

Anita Loos grew up in San Francisco and began acting and writing in her teens. In 1915, she moved to Hollywood, where she earned her living as a screenwriter. At age thirty-one, Loos married movie director and screenwriter John Emerson, but he treated her badly and had many affairs. Her unhappy marriage provided material for her best-selling novel *Gentlemen Prefer Blondes*. During her long career, Loos wrote novels, articles, plays, and short stories as well as dozens of screenplays, including the script for the 1928 movie version of *Gentlemen Prefer Blondes*.

LOVE SONG

"Gee, but it's tough to be broke, kid,
It's not a joke, kid, it's a curse.
My luck is changing, it's gotten,
From something rotten,
To something worse. . . .

I can't give you anything but love, baby.
That's the only thing I've plenty of, baby.
Dream a while, scheme a while,
You're sure to find happiness and, I guess,
All those things you've always longed for."

Lyrics by Dorothy Field from "I Can't Give You Anything But Love," written in 1928 and a hit throughout the Depression years

composer Jerome Kern on the scores of several successful shows, including *Swing Time,* the lead number of which, "The Way You Look Tonight," earned the Academy Award for Best Song in 1936.

Singing and dancing stars such as Marilyn Miller, Vivienne Segal, and Ethel Merman attracted huge audiences to Broadway musicals. Merman had an incredibly powerful voice and was considered to be the queen of musical comedy. Her hits included "I Got Rhythm" and "Anything Goes."

COUNTRY MUSIC

Traditional American music became very popular in the 1920s, especially country music from the southern states. One of the first country acts to gain national fame was the Carter family from

Below: Ethel Merman, "the First Lady of the musical comedy stage," performs with four sailors in the movie version of the musical *Anything Goes.*

Virginia. The group was made up of A. P. Carter, his wife, Sara, and his eighteen-year-old sister-in-law, Maybelle Addington Carter. They began recording traditional country songs in the 1920s, and Maybelle's style of guitar "fingerpicking" was especially admired. Another early country music star was Patsy Montana from Arkansas. In 1935, she released the single "I Want to Be a Cowboy's Sweetheart," which was an instant hit, making her the first female country performer to have a million-selling single.

SINGING SISTERS

In the 1930s, several groups of sisters performed popular songs in close harmony, making use of jazz rhythms and melodies. The earliest of these groups was the Boswell Sisters from New Orleans, who made recordings and performed on national radio. Other singing groups were the Three X Sisters, the Pickens Sisters, and the Andrews Sisters from Minnesota. The Andrews Sisters started out as imitators of the Boswells, singing with dance bands and touring in vaudeville. In 1937, they made their first recordings and radio broadcasts and by 1940 were world famous.

NOVELISTS

During the period from 1921 to 1937, some outstanding novels by women were published. Edith Wharton had been writing novels since 1900 and continued until 1938, when she was in her seventies. Her books describe the lives of the upper classes in New York in the opening decades of the 20th century. In 1921, Wharton

Right: The Boswell Sisters made their first record in 1925. They were one of the first groups to perform vocal jazz.

> **COWBOY SONG**
>
> "I want to be a cowboy's sweetheart
> I want to learn to rope and ride
> I want to ride through the plains and the desert
> Out west of the Great Divide
> I want to hear the coyotes singing
> As the sun sets in the west
> I want to be a cowboy's sweetheart
> That's the life I love the best."
>
> Lyrics from "I Want to Be a Cowboy's Sweetheart," Patsy Montana's country hit of 1935

45

won the Pulitzer Prize for Literature for *The Age of Innocence* (published in 1920), becoming the first woman to win the award.

Another Pulitzer winner was Pearl S. Buck, who was awarded the prize in 1932 for *The Good Earth*, a novel set in China. It was the best-selling work of fiction in the United States in 1931 and 1932, and in 1938 Buck became the first American woman to be awarded the Nobel Prize for Literature. A more romantic writer who also achieved massive sales was Margaret Mitchell. Her novel *Gone With the Wind* was set at the time of the American Civil War and focused on the story of Scarlett

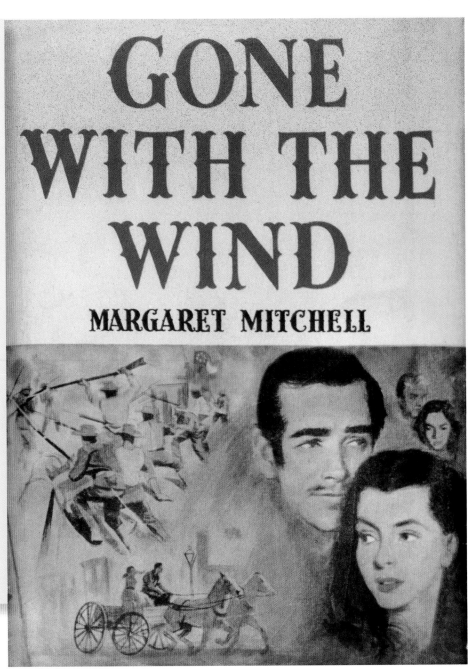

BREAKTHROUGH BIOGRAPHY

MARGARET MITCHELL (1900–49)

Margaret Mitchell lived all her life in Atlanta, Georgia. She married twice, the first time unhappily. Unlike most white southern women, she had a part-time job, writing a column for the local newspaper. Mitchell started writing a Civil War story in 1926 while she was recovering from a broken ankle, and she continued working on it for her own amusement over the next four years. Five years later, in 1935, a visiting publisher asked her if she had ever written any stories, and she showed him the unfinished manuscript. He persuaded her to complete it, and it was published as *Gone With the Wind* the following year.

Right: Margaret Mitchell's romantic novel *Gone With the Wind* was a runaway popular success but also won praise from some literary critics. It was awarded the Pulitzer Prize for Literature in 1937.

O'Hara, the spoiled daughter of a southern plantation owner. *Gone With the Wind* was published in 1936. It was 1,037 pages long and retailed for the unusually high price of three dollars, but sales still reached a million within six months.

POETS

Female poets of the 1920s and 1930s included Hilda Doolittle, Gertrude Stein, and Edna St. Vincent Millay. Doolittle and Stein were part of the experimental "modernist" movement, which included male poets such as T. S. Eliot and Ezra Pound. In their poetry, they tried to break free from conventional verse forms and used strikingly modern images. Millay wrote more traditional, lyrical poems. In 1923, her collection *The Harp-Weaver, and Other Poems* won the Pulitzer Prize for Poetry, the first time the prize had been awarded to a woman.

DOROTHY PARKER AND THE VICIOUS CIRCLE

Dorothy Parker was a poet, writer, and critic who was admired and feared for her witty but bitingly cruel comments. She wrote poems, stories, and theater reviews for a range of New York magazines and published three volumes of poetry and several short story collections. In the 1930s, she began working as a freelance screenwriter and wrote scripts for more than fifteen movies. She also began her involvement in left-wing politics, supporting the revolutionary party in the Spanish Civil War and campaigning against fascism.

Between the years 1919 and 1929, Parker belonged to the Algonquin Round Table, a group of writers, actors, and critics who met for lunch almost daily at Manhattan's Algonquin Hotel. The group, who called themselves "the Vicious Circle," swapped gossip, wordplay, and jokes, and their comments were often published in newspapers and magazines.

Right: Dorothy Parker had a troubled private life and was married three times—twice to the same man.

WITTY WORDS

"The first thing I do in the morning is brush my teeth and sharpen my tongue."

Dorothy Parker

Above: Inspired by the scenery of New Mexico, Georgia O'Keeffe created her own semi-abstract style.

BREAKTHROUGH BIOGRAPHY

**GEORGIA O'KEEFFE
(1887–1986)**

Georgia O'Keeffe grew up on a farm in Wisconsin before studying art and becoming a school art teacher. In 1915, she began to develop her own personal style in a series of bold abstract drawings. These drawings were greatly admired by photographer Alfred Stieglitz, who encouraged O'Keeffe to hold exhibitions and experiment with painting and drawing. In 1924, O'Keeffe and Stieglitz married. The couple lived in New York until Stieglitz's death in 1946, but they took frequent trips to New Mexico. In 1949, O'Keeffe moved permanently to New Mexico, where her work was inspired by the region's plants and landscape.

GEORGIA O'KEEFFE

The outstanding female artist of the period was painter Georgia O'Keeffe. Unlike many American artists of the time, she did not copy European styles of painting. Instead, she created a distinctive style of her own, inspired by the buildings, plants, and landscape of the United States. In the 1920s, O'Keeffe painted pictures of city skyscrapers, but by the 1930s, she was concentrating on giant images of plants, painted in vivid colors and transformed into semi-abstract compositions.

SCULPTORS

The period 1920 to 1940 was an exciting time for women sculptors. Since the 1880s, Adelaide Johnson had been producing powerful portraits of women. In 1921, she completed her most famous work,

48

the Capital Suffrage Monument. It featured carvings of the heads of three suffrage pioneers emerging from a rough block of marble.

Malvina Hoffman created life-size figures in bronze, marble, and plaster. In 1930, she began a major project for Chicago's Field Museum of Natural History, sculpting figures of people from around the world. The finished project consisted of more than a hundred sculptures. Augusta Savage also sculpted powerful figures. She was an African American who played a vital part in the Harlem Renaissance, both as a teacher and as a practicing artist.

PHOTOGRAPHERS

Women also did pioneering work in the field of photography. In the 1920s, Imogen Cunningham produced close-up studies of plants. Later in the decade, she created striking images of industrial landscapes before moving on to photographs of hands.

Margaret Bourke White started her career as a commercial photographer of buildings but in 1929 became a photojournalist, working for a range of news magazines. During the 1930s, Bourke White photographed drought victims in the Dust Bowl. She also took photos showing the rise of the Nazis in Europe and the rule of Stalin in Russia.

Like Margaret Bourke White, Dorothea Lange recorded the effects of the Great Depression. In the 1930s, she was employed by the U.S. government to photograph the farmers of the Dust Bowl. Her powerful photographs reveal the suffering of the homeless men, women, and children who traveled from place to place in search of work and food.

Right: Dorothea Lange's photograph "Migrant Mother" was taken in 1936 in Nipomo, California. It became the most famous image of the Depression years.

" IMAGE OF THE DUST BOWL

"I saw and approached the hungry and desperate mother, as if drawn by a magnet. . . . She told me her age, that she was thirty-two. She said that they had been living on frozen vegetables from the surrounding fields, and birds that the children killed. She had just sold the tires from her car to buy food."

Dorothea Lange describes her meeting with the woman who was the subject of her famous photograph "Migrant Mother"

CHAPTER 7

MINORITY GROUPS

I N THE 1920S AND 1930S LIFE WAS VERY TOUGH FOR MANY WOMEN. African Americans, Native Americans, and Hispanics all faced prejudice and unfair treatment, and the Great Depression hit these groups especially hard. However, some determined women stood up for their rights. In this period, there was also a great flowering of music and the arts among black Americans.

Above: A poor black woman scoops water from a backyard supply in the slums of Washington, D.C.

UNFAIR TREATMENT

African-American women had to cope with discrimination in many areas of their lives. Public transportation, medical facilities, and social meeting places were usually segregated, with different areas for black people and white people. Schools for black Americans were very badly funded. At work, African Americans often received unfair treatment from white employers, and women were especially badly exploited.

50

Above: Mary McLeod Bethune became a close friend of America's first lady, Eleanor Roosevelt. This photograph shows the two women at the opening session of the National Conference on Problems of the Negro and Negro Youth.

WOMEN OF COURAGE AND CONVICTION

MARY MCLEOD BETHUNE (1875–1955)

Mary McLeod Bethune was born in South Carolina. Both her parents had been slaves and she began working in the fields at age five. She was educated to become a missionary but instead devoted her life to helping her fellow black Americans, especially women and girls. She was married and had one son but she always said that the girls in the schools she founded were her first family. After her death, one journalist wrote, "She gave out faith and hope as if they were pills and she some sort of doctor."

> "

TEST OF CHARACTER

"The true worth of a race must be measured by the character of its womanhood."

Mary McLeod Bethune

Even after 1920, when women won the right to vote, some black voters faced obstacles at the polling booths. For example, in 1925 a group of black women who were registering to vote in Birmingham, Alabama, were attacked and beaten by election officials.

Black women even suffered prejudice in sports. In 1932, runners Louise Stokes and Tidye Pickett were the first black women to qualify for the U.S. Olympic Track-and-Field Team and traveled with the rest of the team to the Olympic site at Los Angeles. During the train journey, they suffered cruel treatment from other team members and, just before the race, were replaced by white runners.

MARY MCLEOD BETHUNE

Some determined women—both black and white—campaigned to improve the lives of African Americans, but one individual stood out from the rest. African American Mary McLeod Bethune devoted her life to supporting black Americans, especially women and girls. In 1904, she set up a pioneering school at Daytona Beach, Florida, which established new standards of education for black girls. In addition to serving as president of many black women's associations, she founded the National Council of Negro Women in 1935, with the aim of improving living conditions for black women and their communities.

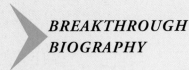

BREAKTHROUGH BIOGRAPHY

JACKIE ORMES (1911–85)

Jackie Ormes was the first African-American woman to publish her cartoons. In the early years of her career, she worked for the *Pittsburgh Courier*, a weekly African-American newspaper. In 1937, Ormes introduced the world of the Harlem Renaissance to a wide audience through her cartoon strip *Torchy Brown in "Dixie to Harlem."* The cartoon told the adventures of Torchy, a black teenage girl from Mississippi, who found fame and fortune singing and dancing in Harlem's famous Cotton Club.

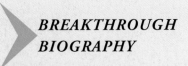

BREAKTHROUGH BIOGRAPHY

ROSE MCCLENDON (1884–1936)

Rose McClendon was a leading black actress. She performed in plays on Broadway and was closely involved in the Harlem Renaissance. As a child, she acted in church plays but did not turn professional until she was in her thirties, when she won a scholarship to drama school. One of her greatest successes was in the play *Mulatto*, by black playwright Langston Hughes. In 1935, she helped to found the Negro People's Theater in Harlem. Tragically, the following year she died from pneumonia at age fifty-two.

As a result of her many campaigns, Bethune was invited to advise the national government on child health and welfare, and from 1936 until 1945, she held an important position in President Roosevelt's administration. As director of Negro Affairs in the National Youth Administration program, Bethune worked tirelessly to secure funding for young black Americans and help them find employment.

WHITE SUPPORT

Some white women gave support to their black "sisters." For example, Mary White Ovington was a member of the board of the National Association of Colored Women, alongside Mary Mcleod Bethune and other black leaders. She was involved in a long legal battle against racial discrimination in housing, education, and employment.

THE HARLEM RENAISSANCE

During the 1920s and 1930s, a group of talented African Americans produced exciting works of literature, art, and music. These writers,

Below: A dancer in a Harlem club, photographed in 1925.

artists, and musicians were mostly based in the Harlem area of New York, and the explosion of culture they created has become known as the Harlem Renaissance. Many of the members of the Harlem Renaissance belonged to the civil rights movement, which campaigned for equal rights for all. Their works express pride in their African roots and a determination to be given equal treatment with whites.

KEY WOMEN

Leaders of the Harlem Renaissance included famous writers and campaigners W. E. B. DuBois and Booker T. Washington, but women also played key roles in the movement. A'Leila Walker was the daughter of self-made businesswoman Madam C. J. Walker. She used her wealth to encourage black writers, setting up a literary "salon" where they could meet in her town house, nicknamed "The Dark Tower."

Jessie Redmon Fauset was literary editor of *The Crisis* magazine from 1919 to 1926. W. E. B. DuBois had launched *The Crisis* with the aim of fighting prejudice and raising awareness of black American rights. Fauset wrote numerous poems, short stories, and articles for the magazine and also published four novels. In 1934, another novelist, Dorothy West, founded *Challenge*, one of the first magazines to publish literature featuring realistic portrayals of African Americans.

Above: Jessie Redmon Fauset was a magazine editor, poet, essayist, and novelist. Her most famous novel, *There Is Confusion* (1924) describes how a black woman at first pretends to be white but later decides to claim her true identity.

NOVELS AND PLAYS

Among the many talented female writers of the Harlem Renaissance were Nella Larsen, Zora Neale Hurston, and Georgia Douglas Camp. Nella Larsen was the first African-American woman to win a Guggenheim Foundation award for creative writing. Her two novels, *Quicksand* (1928) and *Passing* (1929), are portraits of mixed-race women searching for their true identity. Zora Neale Hurston's finest novel, *Their Eyes Were Watching God*, was published in 1937. It portrays

Right: Louis Armstrong (center) and his Hot Five band, photographed in Louisiana in the 1930s. On the far right is Lil Hardin Armstrong, Louis's second wife. Lil was a talented pianist, composer, singer, and bandleader.

> **BREAKTHROUGH BIOGRAPHY**

ELLA FITZGERALD (1917–96)

Ella Fitzgerald's singing career spanned sixty years. She had a hard childhood in New York and spent some of her teenage years in a reform school and an orphanage. In 1934, she made her first stage appearance at age seventeen in an "amateur night" at the Apollo Theater in Harlem. By the following year, she was starring regularly at Harlem's Savoy Ballroom. During the 1930s, she recorded several hit songs, including "Love and Kisses." This marked the start of a brilliant career, which lasted until the 1990s.

a proud, independent black woman who celebrates her heritage and does not feel victimized by it. Georgia Douglas Camp was a poet and playwright. Her most daring play, *A Sunday Morning in the South*, was first performed in 1928. It deals with the lynching of a young innocent black man by corrupt white police.

BLUES AND JAZZ

During the 1920s, the "blues," a form of African-American music that had its origins in the sad but powerful songs sung by slaves on plantations, grew rapidly in popularity. In 1920, Mamie Smith made the first commercial recording of a blues number; this was followed in 1923 by singles by Bessie Smith and Gertrude Rainey. Bessie Smith was the most popular female blues singer of the 1920s and 1930s. Along with Louis Armstrong, she had a major influence on the next generation of singers. Gertrude Rainey was known as "the Mother of the Blues." By 1928, she had made ninety recordings.

At the same time as blues singers were emerging, jazz bands also became very popular. These bands were inspired by the Dixieland performers of New Orleans. Blues singers often sang with the backing of a big band, producing a very exciting sound.

THE JAZZ AGE

By the mid-1920s, jazz had become a passion for white Americans. Bands and singers performed in clubs and bars, and during the Prohibition years (1920–33), jazz was often played in speakeasies. The most famous gathering place for jazz musicians was the Cotton Club in Harlem, New York. Female stars who performed there included Ella Fitzgerald and Billie Holiday. Although the performers at the Cotton Club were black, the audience was white. Black customers were generally not admitted.

GOSPEL SINGERS

In the 1930s, there was a surge of interest in gospel music, sung by African-American church choirs. This was largely the result of the efforts of two people: composer-arranger Thomas A. Dorsey and singer and choir leader Sallie Martin, nicknamed "the mother of gospel music." In 1932, Dorsey and Martin co-founded the National Convention of Gospel Choirs and Choruses, and Martin also formed the Sallie Martin Singers, one of the first all-female gospel groups. Dorsey

Right: Bessie Smith was the highest-paid black entertainer of her day. The press described her as the "Empress of the Blues."

> ## ↻ TURNING POINT
>
> ### DOWNHEARTED BLUES
>
> In 1923, singer Bessie Smith made her first recording, a single of "Downhearted Blues." The record sold 780,000 copies in six months, making her the highest-paid black performer in the United States. "Downhearted Blues" launched Smith's career and became a blues classic. It was included in a list of songs of the century chosen by the Recording Industry of America and is in the Rock and Roll Hall of Fame as one of the 500 songs that shaped rock music.

encouraged individual singers as well as choirs, the best known of whom was Mahalia Jackson. In 1934, Jackson recorded her first album, which included the famous song "God Shall Wipe Away All Tears."

NATIVE AMERICANS

There was a growing interest in Native American culture in the 1920s. This was partly prompted by an important book, published in 1921. *Waheenee: An Indian Girl's Story* describes the life of Buffalo Bird Woman, a member of the Sioux people of North Dakota, as told to the anthropologist Gilbert L. Wilson. The book contains chapters on storytelling, childhood games, and buffalo hunting and describes the changes in traditional life caused by the arrival of white settlers.

HISPANIC AMERICANS

The Mexican Revolution lasted from 1910 to about 1920 and resulted in thousands of refugees crossing the border into the United States. Most of them settled in the southwestern states, especially in the cities

TURNING POINT

NATIVE AMERICAN CITIZENSHIP

In 1924, Congress passed the Indian Citizenship Act, granting full citizenship of the United States to Native Americans. Gaining citizenship meant that Native American men and women had the same rights as other Americans, including the right to vote. However, state governors largely controlled these rights, and many of them allowed Native Americans to be treated as second-class citizens, often denying them the right to vote.

Right: Sioux women with their children photographed in 1925. The women were attending a gathering of Native Americans held at Fort Union, on the border of Montana and North Dakota.

of Los Angeles and San Antonio, Texas. Many refugees faced discrimination in their daily lives and exploitation at work. Despite these hardships, there was a flowering of Hispanic culture in the American Southwest.

In the 1920s, Los Angeles and San Antonio became lively centers for Latin-American musicians, playwrights, and actors. Theater companies toured the Southwest and sometimes traveled across the United States to perform to Hispanic communities in Florida, the Midwest, and New York. One of the leading figures in the Hispanic theater of this period was Mexican actress and director Marita Reid, who founded her own company in 1922. Some Mexican-born actors moved from Hispanic theater to Hollywood. Actress Dolores Del Rio began her Hollywood career with the silent movie *Joanna* in 1925 and went on to star in dozens of films in the 1920s and 1930s.

By the 1930s, Mexican singers and musicians were making their mark in mainstream American culture. In 1934, singer Lydia Mendoza had a big hit with "Mal hombre" and soon became known as *la alondra de la frontera* (the lark of the border). Mexican-born composer Maria Grever composed hundreds of songs, including the hugely popular "Cuando Vuelvo a Tu Lado" (When I Return to Your Side).

Above: Mexican actress Dolores Del Rio was known as "the most beautiful woman of the silent screen."

JEWISH CULTURE

Thousands of Jewish immigrants arrived in the United States in the early decades of the 20th century. Like other minority groups, Jews often faced prejudice and unfair treatment in their new country. Some Jewish writers made a deliberate effort to fight against prejudice by presenting their culture in a humorous way. Actress and scriptwriter Gertrude Edelstein Berg created a popular radio comedy show called *The Goldbergs*, about a Jewish family who moved from New York to Connecticut. The weekly show, starring Berg in the role of the mother, was enormously popular, running from 1929 to 1946.

CULTURAL VIEW

"*I want to show them as they really are—as I, a young Jewish girl, knew them.*"

Gertrude Berg, describing the characters in her radio show *The Goldbergs*.

CHAPTER 8

THE PERIOD IN BRIEF

B Y 1937, WOMEN IN THE UNITED STATES HAD BEEN through good times and bad. In the Roaring Twenties, some young women had experienced new freedoms, but the Great Depression of the 1930s brought hardship and suffering, especially in the Dust Bowl. During the 1920s and 1930s, increasing numbers of women went out to work. In 1920, 8.3 million women had jobs. By 1940, the number of female workers had reached 13 million—25.4 percent of the workforce.

Right: By the late 1930s, large numbers of women were employed in offices. These women are cataloguers in the Library of Congress, Washington, D.C.

TURNING POINT

WOMEN BEHAVING BADLY

In 1926, actress Mae West starred in her first Broadway play, which she also wrote, produced, and directed. The play was called *Sex*, and it was a great success, until the state authorities decided to take action. The New York police were sent to arrest West, and she was sentenced to ten days in jail, but this just added to her popularity. For the next ten years, she continued to shock and delight her audiences in a series of suggestive plays and movies. The staging of *Sex* represented the confident spirit of the 1920s, an era in which some women dared to behave badly.

FEMALE CELEBRITIES

During the years 1921 to 1937, celebrity culture was born in the United States, especially in music, show business, and the movies. Famous stars of this period include actress Mae West, dancer Ginger Rogers, and comedian Fanny Brice. The period also produced some outstanding women in other areas of life. Pilot Amelia Earhart, athlete Babe

Didrikson, dancer Martha Graham, and artist Georgia O'Keeffe all provided inspiring examples of what women could do.

BLACK AMERICANS

By the late 1930s, African-American culture had become part of mainstream American life, thanks to the birth of blues and jazz and the Harlem Renaissance. African-American women such as Bessie Smith and Billie Holiday had become stars, but life was still very hard for the majority of black women, who faced daily discrimination and prejudice.

CHANGING TIMES

By 1937, the United States was beginning to recover from the Great Depression. President Roosevelt's New Deal programs had begun to take effect, and the numbers of unemployed and homeless people had started to fall. However, there was a new danger on the horizon as Hitler gained power in Germany and started planning to invade other countries. World War II began in 1939, and in 1941, the United States joined the conflict. This major world event would have a dramatic impact on the lives of women in the United States.

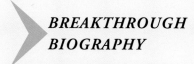

BREAKTHROUGH BIOGRAPHY

BILLIE HOLIDAY (1915–59)

Billie Holiday grew up in poverty in Baltimore and New York. As a teenager she lived and worked in brothels and was arrested several times. In 1929, at age fourteen, Holiday began singing jazz and blues in New York clubs, and in 1933, she made her first recording with Benny Goodman's band. In the late 1930s, she sang with small groups of jazz musicians but also with big bands. Holiday's singing career reached its peak in the 1940s. She had an enormous impact on the development of jazz and introduced a new, deeply personal approach to singing.

Below: In the 1920s and 1930s, the world of sport opened up to women, liberated from their restrictive, old-fashioned clothing. This photograph shows world champion diver Georgia Coleman at the start of a daring double-back somersault.

TIMELINE

1921
Margaret Sanger founds the American Birth Control League.
Lila Acheson Wallace co-founds *Reader's Digest* magazine.
Edith Wharton is the first woman to win the Pulitzer Prize in fiction, for *The Age of Innocence*.
Waheenee: An Indian Girl's Story is published.
The Sheppard-Towner Maternity and Infancy Protection Act is passed.
The Women's Peace Union (WPU) is founded.

1922
Actress Marita Reid forms her own Hispanic theater company.
The Amateur Athletic Union (AAU) adds track-and-field events for women.

1923
Bessie Smith records her first single, "Downhearted Blues." It sells over 800,000 copies.
In the law case *Adkins v. the Children's Hospital*, the U.S. Supreme Court rules against women's right to a minimum wage and in favor of the principle of special protection for women.
Ida Kaganovich Rosenthal founds the Maidenform Brassiere Company.
Edna St. Vincent Millay wins the Pulitzer Prize for Poetry.
Alice Paul proposes the Equal Rights Amendment (ERA) to the U.S. Constitution. It is not passed.

1924
Congress grants full U.S. citizenship to Native Americans.
Artist Georgia O'Keeffe begins making large-scale flower paintings.

1925
Architect Julia Morgan completes San Simeon, William Randolph Hearst's castle in California.
Nellie Tayloe Ross is the first woman to serve as a state governor.

1926
Gertrude Ederle is the first woman to swim the English Channel.
Martha Graham forms the Martha Graham School of Contemporary Dance.
Actress Mae West stars in *Sex*, a scandalous Broadway play, which she also writes, produces, and directs.

1927
Clara Bow appears in the movie *It*. She becomes known as the "It girl."

1928
Women compete for the first time in Olympic track-and-field events.
Anthropologist Margaret Mead publishes *Coming of Age in Samoa*, a study on adolescence and sexuality.

1929
The Wall Street Crash marks the start of the Great Depression.
Armed troops are called in to break a strike of women workers at a rayon plant in Elizabethton, Tennessee.
Labor organizer Ella Mae Wiggins is killed during a textile mill strike in Gastonia, North Carolina.

1930
Pearl S. Buck's first novel, *East Wind: West Wind*, is published.
Ethel Merman begins her successful theater and movie career by singing "I've Got Rhythm" on Broadway.

1931
Jane Addams, founder of the settlement house movement, is the first American woman to win the Nobel Peace Prize.

1932   Amelia Earhart becomes the first woman to fly solo from the United States to Europe.
Hattie Caraway is the first woman elected to the U.S. Senate.
Ruth Nichols is the first woman hired as a pilot for commercial passenger flights.
Athlete "Babe" Didrikson (later Zaharias) wins two gold medals and a silver in Olympic track-and-field events.

1933   Jazz singer Billie Holiday makes her first recording with Benny Goodman's band.
Frances Perkins becomes secretary of labor and the first female member of the federal cabinet.
Connie Smith leads a successful strike of 900 black women pecan workers.
Dancer and actress Ginger Rogers joins Fred Astaire for *Flying Down to Rio*, the first of their nine tap-dancing movies together.
The Los Angeles dressmakers' strike involves roughly 2,000 women, mostly Mexican Americans.

1934   Gangsters Bonnie Parker and Clyde Barrow are shot dead by police.
Dora Jones starts the Domestic Workers' Union.

1935   Actress Rose McClendon helps to found the Negro People's Theater in Harlem.
Patsy Montana is the first female country singer to top a million in record sales with "I Want to Be a Cowboy's Sweetheart."

1936   Mary McLeod Bethune is named director of Negro Affairs of the National Youth Administration.
Margaret Mitchell publishes her best-selling novel *Gone With the Wind*.
Dorothea Lange takes her famous photograph "Migrant Mother."

1937   King Edward VIII abdicates from the British throne in order to marry Wallis Simpson.
Genora Johnson Dollinger organizes women to support the strikers at the General Motors sit-down strike in Flint, Michigan.
Bertha Thompson publishes *The Autobiography of Boxcar Bertha*.
Margaret Fogarty Rudkin starts the multi-million-dollar Pepperidge Farm company.

GLOSSARY AND FURTHER INFORMATION

abstract A style of fine art that shows ideas rather than scenes, objects or figures.

anthropologist Someone who studies the beliefs and ways of life of people around the world.

anthropology The study of the beliefs and ways of life of people around the world.

antibiotic A drug that kills bacteria and is used to fight infections.

amendment An article added to the Constitution.

asthma A medical condition that makes people wheeze and have difficulty breathing.

bilingual Fluent in more than one language.

blues A type of folk music developed by African Americans at the start of the 20th century.

bootlegger Someone who smuggles alcohol. So-called because bootleggers often hid flasks of alcohol in the legs of their boots.

boxcar A large metal container used for transporting goods by rail.

brewery A place where beer is made.

brothel A place where men pay to have sex with prostitutes.

capital punishment Punishment by death.

civil rights People's rights to freedom, safety and protection from discrimination.

communism A way of organizing a country so that all the land and industry belongs to the state and all the profits are shared out among the people.

constitution The basic principles and laws of a nation, state, or social group that determine the powers and duties of the government and guarantee certain rights to the people in it.

contraceptive A device used to prevent pregnancy.

depression A period when the economy is doing badly and many people have no work.

discrimination Treating a particular group in society unfairly, for example, because of their race or sex.

distillery A place where alcoholic drinks, such as whiskey, are made.

fascism A way of organizing a country with a powerful dictator and just one political party so that only some chosen people hold all the power and others are treated very unjustly.

fascist Someone who believes in fascism as a system of government.

federal A system of government in which a country is divided into states, which form a union but which have independent control of their own internal affairs.

Harlem Renaissance An African-American cultural movement that flourished in the 1920s and 1930s in the Harlem district of New York. Members of the Harlem Renaissance were writers, artists, musicians, actors and directors.

hobo An unemployed person who rides the railroads in search of work.

immigrant A person who moves to another country to live.

jurisdiction Laws.

labor union A group of workers who have organized to gain fair working conditions or pay.

militant Aggressive and determined.

nationalist Someone who is proud of his or her country and prepared to fight for its independence.

pediatrics The branch of medicine that is concerned with children.

pharmacist Someone who prepares and sells drugs and medicines.

prejudice Negative feelings toward a group of people that are not based on facts.

psychologist A person whose job it is to study the human mind and its functions, especially in terms of behavior.

progressive In favor of social reform in order to improve people's lives.

Prohibition Law against making or selling liquor.

Quaker A Christian group whose members reject formal services and hold meetings in which anyone may speak. Quakers often campaign for peace and social reform.

radical Having extreme views.

salon A group of writers and other creative people who meet in the home of a wealthy person to exchange ideas.

segregated When people of different races (or religions or sexes) are separated and and treated differently.

shares Portions of the value of a business. People buy shares in a company to help fund it. In return, they receive regular, small amounts of money, depending on how profitable the company is.

stock market An organization responsible for buying and selling shares.

strike A refusal to work, because of a disagreement with an employer.

suffrage The right to vote in public elections, especially elections for local and national leaders.

suffragist Someone who campaigns for the right to vote in elections.

temperance The avoidance of all forms of alcohol.

tycoon A very rich and powerful businessman.

U.S. Mint The place where the U.S. government makes paper money and coins.

vaudeville A form of entertainment consisting of short acts, such as songs and comedy routines.

whooping cough An infectious disease that causes violent coughing and can kill.

BOOKS

Banner, Lois W. *Women in Modern America: A Brief History*. Florence, Kentucky: Wadsworth Publishing, 2004.

Hemming, Heidi, and Julie Savage. *Women Making America*. Silver Spring, Maryland: Clotho Press, 2009.

May, Martha. *Women's Roles in Twentieth-Century America*. Westport, Connecticut: Greenwood, 2009.

Steinbeck, John. *The Grapes of Wrath*. New York: Arrow, 1995 (first published 1939).

DVDS

Bonnie and Clyde (Warner Brothers, 1967) Tells the story of gangsters Bonnie Parker and Clyde Barrow during the period of Prohibition and Depression.

The Grapes of Wrath (20th Century Fox, 1940) A classic film adapted from the novel by John Steinbeck. It follows the fate of migrant farmers from the Dust Bowl trying to find a better life in California.

Modern Times (United Artists, 1936) Charlie Chaplin's famous film is a commentary on the desperate conditions faced by people during the Great Depression.

WEB SITES

http://www.1920-30.com/

americanart.si.edu/exhibitions/online/1934/

xroads.virginia.edu/~1930s/front.html

http://www.okcmoa.com/harlemrenaissance

PLACES TO VISIT

Amelia Earhart Birthplace Museum, Atchison, Kansas
A museum dedicated to the life and achievements of Amelia Earhart, the first woman to fly an aircraft solo across the Atlantic Ocean.

Oakland Museum of California, Oakland, California
Contains a major collection of photographs by Dorothea Lange, mostly taken during the Great Depression.

INDEX